THE
BLESSED

A GATEWAY CHURCH RESOURCE
SECOND EDITION

THE BLESSED LIFE SMALL GROUP STUDY GUIDE

The Blessed Life Small Group Study Guide
Second Edition
Copyright © 2011, 2013 Gateway Church

Printed in the United States of America.

gatewaypeople.com

Contents

It's All About the Heart

WEALTH. MONEY. THINGS. THE WAY WE USE THEM REVEALS
VOLUMES ABOUT OUR ATTITUDES TOWARD POSSESSIONS AND
TOWARD GOD — ATTITUDES THAT ULTIMATELY DETERMINE
THE QUALITY OF OUR STEWARDSHIP AND OUR ABILITY TO
EXPERIENCE THE BLESSED LIFE.

Engage

What is the most selfless thing you've ever seen anyone do?

-OR-

What is the most unselfish thing anyone has ever done for you?

Watch Robert Morris' teaching titled "It's All About the Heart." As you view it:

- Look for four key action steps that launch you on the road to blessing and joy-filled usefulness in God's kingdom.

- Watch for the key to his personal stewardship testimony.

(If you are not able to watch this teaching on DVD, read the following pages. Otherwise, skip to the TALK section after viewing.)

READ

Luke 6:38 is a wonderful verse of scripture. But it is also one of the most frequently misapplied and misunderstood verses in the Bible.

Its words are very familiar to most Christians. You can probably quote it from memory: "Give, and it will be given to you: good measure, pressed down, shaken together, and running over will be put into your bosom. For with the same measure that you use, it will be measured back to you" (NKJV).

One of the most common mistakes people make about this verse is assuming that Jesus is speaking only of money. In truth, He's revealing a principle that applies to every area of our lives.

This becomes crystal clear if you look at the larger context of the verse. For instance,

> THE FACT IS, GOD DOESN'T BLESS GIVING.
>
> HE BLESSES GIVING FROM A RIGHT HEART ATTITUDE.

back up a couple of verses and look at verses 36 and 37: "Therefore be merciful, just as your Father also is merciful. Judge not, and you shall not be judged. Condemn not, and you shall not be condemned. Forgive, and you will be forgiven."

It is only then that Jesus says, "Give and it will be given to you" (v. 38). Yes, this principle applies to money, but you can also give forgiveness. You can give mercy. You can give understanding, patience, time, or service.

Jesus is simply talking about the broad principle of giving. Whatever you give is going to be given back to you in "good measure, pressed down, shaken together, and running over."

Think about it this way. When you give away an apple seed by planting it, you don't just get back an apple seed. In time, you actually get back a whole apple tree, and on that tree are many apples, and each apple has many seeds. You get back so much more than you actually give. This is a fundamental principle of the kingdom of God. It is a truth that has been called the *law of reciprocity.*

Yet this is precisely where so many people go wrong regarding this passage of Scripture. Once you understand the wonderful truth of it, there is a tremendous temptation to make it your motivation for giving.

The basic problem with most teaching about giving based upon Luke 6:38 is that material gain is presented as the primary motive for giving. God doesn't want us to catch the vision of getting. He wants us to catch the vision of giving.

God is a giver. And, yes, it's true that when we give, God will ensure that we are blessed. But that should not be our motive for giving. We should give for the pure joy of imitating our wonderful Father.

It's our hearts the Lord is concerned about.

IT'S OUR HEARTS THE LORD IS CONCERNED ABOUT.

Deuteronomy 15:7-15 directly addresses these matters of the heart where generosity and giving are concerned. There, God's people are exhorted to give liberally and willingly to those who need help. In verse 10 we read: "You shall surely give to him, **and your heart should not be grieved when you give to him,** because for this thing the LORD your God will bless you in all your works and in all to which you put your hand" [emphasis added].

4 points:
1. Deal w/a selfish heart. Dt. 15:9
2. Deal w/a grieving heart. Dt. 15:10
3. Develop a generous heart. Dt. 15:15
4. Develop a grateful heart. Dt. 15:15

Here is clear evidence that God looks at the heart attitude of the giver. He makes it a point to tell the Israelites not to let their hearts "be grieved" when they give. All the way back then, God loved "a cheerful giver." (2 Corinthians 9:7)

The fact is, God doesn't bless giving. He blesses giving from a right heart attitude.

At the end of that passage in Deuteronomy 15, the Word says, "From what the LORD your God has blessed you with, you shall give to him. You shall remember that you were a slave in the land of Egypt, and the LORD your God redeemed you; therefore I command you this thing today" (vv. 14-15).

Why did God create giving?
"to work selfishness & greed out of our life."

Why did God instruct the Israelites to remember that they had been slaves? Because it would fill their hearts with gratitude for what He had done for them.

When we allow God to remind us that we used to be slaves to sin and that everything we have is by His gracious hand, it will help us to be grateful. And when we're grateful, it's easy to be generous.

Genuine gratitude to God is a rare and powerful thing. And a heart of gratitude is a vital key to cultivating a lifestyle of generosity.

NOTES

Mt. 7:1-2
Lk 6:37-38 → Reward for giving
w/ the right heart.
- Jesus is talking @ the condition
of our heart.
- It depends upon what you give -
love, judgement, money, etc.
you will get it back!
Dt. 15:7-15

Generosity comes from
Gratitude.

Talk

For group discussion or personal reflection:

Judge not . . . Condemn not . . . Forgive . . .
Give, and it will be given to you . . . pressed
down, shaken together, and running over
(Luke 6:37, 38).

QUESTION 1

This passage obviously speaks of much
more than just money. Some have called
this the "Spiritual Law of Reciprocity" —
whatever you give (judgment, mercy, time,
service) will be returned to you in abun-
dance. What are some areas of your life
in which you have seen this "sowing and
reaping" principle at work in the past —
for either good or for bad?

QUESTION 2

"Giving to get" seems to have become the
standard approach in motivating believers
to share. In what ways does the declaration
"God doesn't bless giving; He blesses giving
with the right heart," challenge what you
have been taught in the past about giving?

> "JUDGE NOT . . .
> CONDEMN NOT
> . . . FORGIVE . . .
> GIVE, AND IT WILL
> BE GIVEN TO YOU
> . . . PRESSED
> DOWN, SHAKEN
> TOGETHER, AND
> RUNNING OVER."
>
> LUKE 6:37, 38

QUESTION 3

When giving produces grief in your soul, it is an indicator that you considered that resource "yours." Have you felt grief or regret after giving an offering to the Lord? What are some ways to help keep yourself mindful of your status as a steward rather than an owner?

QUESTION 4

More people struggle with tithing than seemingly any other principle in Scripture. Why do you think this is so? What are some common emotional and mental barriers to being obedient in this area?

QUESTION 5

Generosity flows easily and naturally from a heart of gratitude. What are some practical ways to cultivate a more grateful heart toward God?

Explore

Want to go deeper? Here is some food for thought, prayer, and journaling in the coming week.

KEY QUOTE
"Generosity comes from gratitude. When you realize that everything you have came from God, it's easy to give it back to Him."
—Robert Morris

Ask the Holy Spirit to show you the trajectory of your life without Christ. In other words, how would that life be different from the one you have now?

_____

_____

_____

_____

"GRATITUDE IS WHAT PRODUCES GENEROSITY . . . WHEN YOU ALLOW THE LORD TO REMIND YOU [OF ALL HE HAS DELIVERED YOU FROM]."

— ROBERT MORRIS

"Father, of all that you have done for me, I am especially grateful for . . ."

_____

_____

_____

KEY VERSES
Deuteronomy 15:7-15, Malachi 3:8-12, Matthew 6:21, Luke 6:37, 38

What is the Holy Spirit saying to you through these scriptures?

_____

_____

_____

_____

KEY QUESTION

If your heart tends to gravitate toward those things you have invested most heavily in, what does your discretionary spending say about your passions and priorities? And vice versa?

_____

_____

_____

_____

_____

WHERE IS MY MONEY GOING?

My top five categories of discretionary spending (e.g. eating out, entertainment, ministry giving, travel, recreation, etc.)

CATEGORY	AVERAGE MONTHLY SPENDING
1. _____	$ _____
2. _____	$ _____
3. _____	$ _____
4. _____	$ _____
5. _____	$ _____

KEY PRAYER

Father, please help me cultivate a grateful heart toward You. Remind me all You have done for me and all You have delivered me from. May it produce in me a lifestyle of generosity and the grace of giving.

What Test?

TITHING—OFFERING TO GOD THE FIRST TENTH OF OUR INCREASE OR INCOME—IS THOROUGHLY BIBLICAL. FURTHERMORE, IT IS A PROFOUNDLY SIGNIFICANT TEST OF OUR LOVE FOR, TRUST IN, AND OBEDIENCE TO OUR HEAVENLY FATHER.

Engage

RECAP

In the previous segment, we were encouraged to examine ourselves for traces of a selfish or "grieving" heart where material things are concerned and to meditate on all God has done for us in order to cultivate a posture of heart-gratitude.

Describe any moments this week in which these issues came to mind. Have you been presented with an opportunity to walk in generosity? If so, how did you respond?

ENGAGE

A commonly reported nightmare is a dream in which you are back in school and discover—to your horror—that an important test is being given, you're very late, and you haven't pre-pared! Why do you think so many people have this dream? Do you have a stressful or funny recurring dream?

TITHING IS NOT A BURDEN. IT'S A BENEFIT.

Watch Robert Morris' teaching titled "What Test?" As you view it:

• Look for the practical definition of the Bible word "ordinance."

• Listen for three key truths about tithing.

(If you are not able to watch this teaching on DVD, read the following pages. Otherwise, skip to the TALK section after viewing.)

READ

Tithing represents a test for every believer. The word translated "tithe" in the Bible literally means "tenth" or "a tenth part." Many people don't realize that the number ten, as used in the Bible, is rich with symbolic significance. Just as recurring numbers such as seven and forty carry special meaning, the same is true with the number ten.

Ten is consistently associated with "testing" in Scripture. For example, in the book of Exodus, Pharaoh's heart was tested by ten plagues. God's standard of righteousness (which tests our conduct) was delivered in the form of Ten Commandments. The children of Israel experienced ten specific tests or trials while wandering in the wilderness.

In the book of Genesis, we find young Jacob working for his future father-in-law Laban. In that season, Jacob's loyalty and character were tested ten times in the form of unjust changes in his wages. And in the first chapter of the book that bears his name, Daniel is tested for ten days.

This pattern continues right into the New Testament. In Matthew 25, ten virgins are tested for their preparedness. Ten days of testing are mentioned in Revelation 2:10.

Given this pattern of meaning surrounding the number ten, it shouldn't come as a surprise to learn that tithing (giving a tenth of our increase back to God) represents a key test for the child of God. But it also represents a test for God! As the Lord declares in Malachi 3:10:

*"Bring the whole tithe into the storehouse, so that there may be food in My house, **and test Me now in this**," says the LORD of hosts, "if I will not open for you the windows of heaven and pour out for you a blessing until it overflows"* [NASB, emphasis added].

Tithing is not a burden. It's a benefit. Furthermore, this passage about tithing is the only place in God's Word in which we are encouraged to "test" God. At the same time, the tithe represents the ultimate heart test for the believer.

Look at this passage in context and it becomes even clearer that the choice for the Christian is a straightforward choice between blessings and curses, not unlike the one Moses put before the Israelites as they prepared to enter the Promised Land:

I call heaven and earth as witnesses today against you, that I have set before you life and death, blessing and cursing; therefore choose life, that both you and your descendants may live (Deuteronomy 30:19).

A similar choice belongs to the believer in relation to tithing. God immediately precedes his promise of opening "the windows of heaven" for the tither by saying: "Will a man rob God? Yet you have robbed Me! But you say, 'In what way have we robbed You?' In tithes and offerings. You are cursed with a curse" (Malachi 3:8, 9).

This is obviously a serious matter to the Lord. Yet some resist this teaching and argue that New Testament believers cannot possibly experience a curse in their finances because Jesus bore the curse of sin for us all on the cross.

There is indeed a wonderful spiritual truth in the words of Galatians 3:13, 14:

Christ has redeemed us from the curse of the law, having become a curse for us (for it is written, "Cursed is everyone who hangs on a tree"), that the blessing of Abraham might come upon the Gentiles in Christ Jesus, that we might receive the promise of the Spirit through faith.

Without a doubt, Jesus bore more than we can possibly imagine on the cross. But consider the following verse—1 Peter 2:24, speaks of Jesus and His sacrifice: "who Himself bore our sins in His own body on the tree, that we, having died to sins, might live for righteousness—by whose stripes you were healed." The verse clearly declares that Jesus bore our sins on the cross. But have you sinned since you became a be-

> CLEARLY, IT IS POSSIBLE TO EXPERIENCE THE EFFECTS OF THE CURSE, EVEN THOUGH CHRIST TOOK THOSE EFFECTS FULLY UPON HIMSELF. WE MUST ALL APPROPRIATE BY FAITH WHAT JESUS DID FOR US ON THE CROSS.

liever? This verse (and others) also proclaims the wonderful truth that Jesus bore our sicknesses in His body through His suffering. But have you been sick since becoming a Christian?

Clearly, it is possible to experience the effects of the curse, even though Christ took those effects fully upon Himself. We must all appropriate by faith what Jesus did for us on the cross. And when we don't, we continue to experience some of the effects of the curse.

If we disobey the Word of God as believers, we can and do experience the negative consequences of sin. This applies to our finances just as surely as it applies to our physical bodies. Can we, if we are in willful violation of God's principles of firstfruits and the tithe, see our finances come under a curse? Yes, we can.

Will God bless the faithful steward who passes the test by honoring Him with the tithe from a grateful heart? Test Him and find out!

NOTES

For group discussion or personal reflection:

QUESTION 1

Through disobedience to God's precepts, it is possible to step out from under God's protective umbrella of favor and protection. Perhaps you have experienced that in some area of your life other than finances. If you are comfortable talking about it, what were the consequences and what did you do to realign your life with God's Word and will?

[T]hen you shall say before the LORD your God: 'I have removed the holy tithe from my house . . . [therefore] Look down from Your holy habitation, from heaven, and bless Your people (Deuteronomy 26:13, 15).

QUESTION 2

In praying for God's blessings on a certain area of your life, what happens to your level of faith and confidence when you know you have been obedient to the Word in that area?

QUESTION 3

Read 1 John 3:18-22. What does this passage indicate about the link between our obedience, our confidence in prayer before God, and the results we get? What is the cure for a condemning heart according to 1 John 1:9?

QUESTION 4

Hebrews 7:8 suggests that when we tithe here on earth, Jesus spiritually receives those tithes in heaven. How does that knowledge impact your heart attitude as you bring your tithes and offerings?

QUESTION 5

Have you tended to view tithing as a burden or a benefit? What practical steps could you take to keep yourself mindful of the benefits of tithing?

PRAY

Take some time as a group to lift one another up in the light of the truths discussed in this session.

Want to go deeper? Here is some food for thought, prayer, and journaling in the coming week.

KEY QUOTE

"Let me tell you what you are telling Jesus every time you get paid. You're telling Him how much you think of Him. You're telling Him how much you love Him."
— Robert Morris

Write a note to Jesus expressing how you feel about Him.

Dear Lord Jesus,

_____

_____

_____

_____

_____

_____

Does what you expressed above align with the message you consistently send through your giving?

_____

_____

_____

KEY VERSES

Malachi 3:8-12, II Chronicles 31:4, Deuteronomy 15:20, Matthew 5:17-20, Matthew 23:23, Hebrews 7:8, 1 John 3:18-22

What stands out to you as you read these verses?

_____

_____

_____

_____

What is the Holy Spirit saying to you through these scriptures?

_____

_____

_____

_____

KEY QUESTION

Given that tithing is a test, what—according to your understanding of the Word—are the benefits of passing that test?

_____

_____

_____

_____

KEY PRAYER

Father, please give me the courage, trust and faith in Your goodness to bring the whole tithe into Your storehouse. Give me the fuller revelation that when I tithe, Jesus Himself receives it. And grace me with a sensitive, generous heart that promptly responds when Your Holy Spirit nudges me to give and share of the resources with which You have entrusted me.

The Principle of First

THE PRINCIPLE OF FIRSTFRUITS IS A UNIVERSAL AND ETERNAL
SPIRITUAL PRECEPT. WE NEED TO DISCOVER THE POWER OF
PUTTING GOD FIRST.

Engage

RECAP

In the previous section, we discussed that although we can't earn God's favor or love, obedience to the Word nevertheless produces confidence before God. This in turn produces more power in prayer (1 John 3:21).

In your prayer times this week, were you aware of your level of confidence before God? Did you make any new choices regarding your obedience in the area of finances?

ENGAGE

"Firsts" are always memorable. A first trip overseas. Your first paying job. The first baby you bring home from the hospital. Share a brief story about one of these "firsts" and why it was so special or interesting?

Watch Robert Morris' teaching titled "The Principle of First" As you view it:

• Look for three important spiritual truths about "first" things.

• Watch for the key heart element that firstfruits offerings require.

(If you are not able to watch this teaching on DVD, read the following pages. Otherwise, skip to the TALK section after viewing.)

READ

Only those of a certain age will remember the old comedy team of Abbott and Costello and their most famous sketch called "Who's On First?" Of course, we've all heard the old saying: "First things first."

So what are the "first things" where living the blessed life are concerned? Consider this: There are more than 500 verses in the Bible concerning prayer and nearly 500 verses concerning faith. But there are more than 2,000 verses relating to money and possessions.

The very first principle we must grasp if we are to understand giving is the principle of *firstfruits*. It can also be called the principle of the *firstborn* or simply the *tithe*.

Frankly, far too many Christians are confused about tithing and the principle of firstfruits. We find an important financial precedent established in Exodus 13:2.

GOD PLAINLY DECLARES THAT THE FIRSTBORN IS "MINE." IT BELONGS TO HIM. IN FACT, SIXTEEN TIMES IN SCRIPTURE, YOU'LL FIND GOD DECLARING THAT THE FIRSTBORN IS HIS!

In this passage, God says, "Consecrate to Me all the firstborn, whatever opens the womb among the children of Israel, both of man and beast; it is Mine."

Here, God plainly declares that the firstborn is "Mine." It belongs to Him. In fact, sixteen times in Scripture, you'll find God declaring that the firstborn is His! For example, Exodus 13:12, 13 says:

that you shall set apart to the Lord all that open the womb, that is, every firstborn that comes from an animal which you have; the males shall be the LORD's. But every firstborn of every donkey you shall redeem with a lamb; and if you will not redeem it, then you shall break its neck. And all the firstborn of man among your sons you shall redeem.

It is vital to understand something about the principle of the firstborn. According to Old Testament law, the firstborn was to be either sacrificed or redeemed. There was no third option. Every time one of your livestock animals delivered its firstborn, you were to sacrifice it. If it was designated an unclean animal (a donkey, for example), you had to redeem it with a clean, spotless lamb. To summarize, the clean firstborn had to be sacrificed and the unclean firstborn had to be redeemed.

With that in mind, think about the account in the New Testament in which John the Baptist meets Jesus on the banks of the Jordan River.

John was baptizing one day and looked up to see Jesus walking toward him. At that point, John cried out, "Behold! The Lamb of God who takes away the sin of the world!" (John 1:29).

With that inspired declaration, John perfectly defined the role Jesus had come to fulfill. Jesus was God's firstborn. Jesus was clean—perfect and unblemished in every way. On the other hand, every one of us was born unclean. We were all born sinners with a fully active sin nature.

> IT'S BEEN SAID THAT GOD ENSURES ANY FIRST THING GIVEN IS NEVER LOST. IN OTHER WORDS, WHAT WE GIVE TO GOD WE DON'T LOSE, BECAUSE GOD REDEEMS IT FOR US.

Now think back to the principle of the firstborn in Exodus. The Law stated that if the firstborn animal were clean, it was to be sacrificed. But if the firstborn were unclean, it was to be redeemed with a clean animal.

Do you see the symbolic parallel? Jesus Christ was God's spotless lamb. But every one of us was born unclean; therefore, Jesus was sacrificed to redeem us.

When He redeemed us by His sacrifice, He bought us back for God. He was literally a firstfruits offering. In a very real sense, Jesus was God's tithe. Is it any wonder the tithe is such a serious and holy thing with God?

God gave His tithe (Jesus) in faith before we ever believed. Romans 5:8 says, "But God demonstrates His own love toward us, in that while we were still sinners, Christ died for us."

We have to give our firstfruits offering—our tithe—in much the same way. Before we see the blessing of God, we give it in faith. Before we know if we're going to have any "month left over at the end of our money," we give in faith and trust.

God didn't wait to see if we would first change or repent or make ourselves worthy. God initiated the principle of first things first.

The principle of the firstfruits is very significant and important to God. It's been said that God ensures that any first thing given is never lost. In other words, what we give to God we don't lose, because God redeems it for us. But what we withhold from God, we will lose. Jesus echoed this principle when He said, For whoever wants to save their life will lose it, but whoever loses his life for My sake will find it. (Matthew 16:25 NIV)

The first belongs to God. We find this principle throughout God's Word. We can give God the first of our time. Likewise, we can give Him the first of our finances. That's what tithing really is—giving our first to God. It's saying, "God, I'm going to give to You first and trust You to redeem the rest."

Put another way, when a firstborn lamb is born in a flock, it is not possible to know how many more lambs that ewe will produce. Nevertheless, God didn't say, "Let your ewe produce nine lambs first and then give Me the next one." No, God says, "Give me the first one."

It always requires faith to give the first. That's why so few Christians experience the blessings of tithing. It requires giving to God before you see if you're going to have enough. By tithing, it is as if we are saying to God, "I recognize You first. I am putting You first in my life, and I trust You to take care of the rest of the things in my life."

As with most other matters in the Christian life, it

comes down to the attitude of our hearts. The question is, "Do I trust God enough to give the first part to Him?"

It's a vital question because God has woven the principle of firstfruits into the spiritual fabric of creation itself. That principle declares: The first portion is the redemptive portion. And when that first portion is given to God, the rest is redeemed.

Acknowledging this principle means confronting with gut-level honesty a very important, very personal question . . .

Who's really first in my life?

NOTES

_____

_____

_____

_____

_____

_____

_____

_____

_____

_____

_____

_____

Talk

For group discussion or personal reflection:

QUESTION 1

Every time we are paid, an inescapable moment of "worship" immediately follows. The first place to which we direct a portion of that money reveals something about what is "first" in our lives. What kinds of financial things are most likely to compete for "first place" in our hearts?

QUESTION 2

A true firstfruits sacrifice or offering requires faith. Typically, what sorts of thoughts, fears, or doubts try to undermine that kind of faith?

There is one who scatters, yet increases more;
And there is one who withholds more than
is right, But it leads to poverty (Proverbs 11:24).

QUESTION 3

God ensures that any *first thing* given to Him is never lost. But as the verse above reminds us, what we unjustly withhold from God, we will lose. In what ways have you seen this principle at work in your life or the life of someone close to you?

_____

_____

_____

QUESTION 4

From God's perspective, why would bringing the *first* tenth of your paycheck be any different than tithing a full 10% *after* all your bills are paid?

_____

_____

_____

QUESTION 5

A 2007 survey by the Barna organization revealed that among Americans who had "prayed, read the Bible, and attended a church service in the previous week," only 12% made a regular practice of tithing. Why do you think that this one area proves so diffi-cult for Bible-believing, church-going people?

_____

_____

_____

PRAY

Take some time as a group to lift one another up in the light of the truths discussed in this session.

Want to go deeper? Here is some food for thought, prayer, and journaling in the coming week.

KEY QUOTE

"If God gave us His first and best [Jesus], why wouldn't we give Him our first and best?" —Robert Morris

We all have areas in which we find it easier to trust the Lord and other areas in which we seem to struggle to rest in His promises. Respond to the following prompts.

I find it easy to trust God about . . .

_____

_____

_____

_____

_____

Sometimes I struggle to trust God concerning . . .

_____

_____

_____

_____

KEY VERSES

Exodus 13:1, 2:11-16, Matthew 16:25, Proverbs 3:9, 10, Romans 11:16, 1 Corinthians 15:20-23, 1 Corinthians 16:1, 2

What stands out to you as you read these verses?

_____

_____

_____

_____

What is the Holy Spirit saying to you through these scriptures?

_____

_____

_____

_____

_____

KEY QUESTION

In practical, real-world terms, how could the principle of firstfruits be applied to your time rather than your money?

_____

_____

_____

_____

KEY PRAYER

Father, You gave Your first and best—Your only Son—so that I could be redeemed. Thank you. Now help me honor Your sacrifice by consistently bringing You the first and best of my time, my talent, and my financial increase.

Breaking the Spirit of Mammon

MAMMON ISN'T ANOTHER NAME FOR MONEY. IT IS A SPIRIT WHICH CAN REST UPON MONEY IF OUR STEWARDSHIP PRIORITIES ARE OUT OF ORDER.

RECAP

In the previous section, we talked about the eternal spiritual principle of *firstfruits*.

In the past week, did you encounter any opportunities to show God that He is first in your life? Did doing so test your level of trust in His faithfulness and goodness?

ENGAGE

One study showed that 70% of lottery winners squander their wealth within a few years. And a recent documentary explored the fact that many people who win the lottery find that sudden, unearned wealth utterly ruins their lives. Why do you think this is the case?

Watch

Watch Robert Morris' teaching titled "Breaking the Spirit of Mammon." As you view it:

• Look for the reason many believers end up "despising" God because of their finances.

• Watch for the link between the spirit of mammon and the Antichrist.

(If you are not able to watch this teaching on DVD, read the following pages. Otherwise, skip to the TALK section after viewing.)

READ

Begin by reading Luke 16:9-16 (NKJV).

You may recognize "mammon" as a word that appears four times in the New Testament. Three of those occurrences are in the passage you just read. The other is in a parallel passage in Matthew.

Jesus' use of the word "mammon" as a name here indicates that He is talking about some kind of demonic spirit or false god. Furthermore, Jesus clearly suggests that it is *possible* to serve mammon instead of serving God, but He goes even further. Jesus states it is *impossible* to serve both at the same time.

He says that you will love the one and hate the other. You will be loyal to one and despise the other. But just what is mammon? "Mammon" is an Aramaic word that essen-

DID YOU KNOW THAT ALL MONEY HAS SOME KIND OF SPIRIT ON IT? IT EITHER HAS THE SPIRIT OF GOD ON IT BECAUSE IT HAS BEEN REDEEMED AND SANCTIFIED OR IT HAS THE SPIRIT OF MAMMON.

tially means "riches." And apparently, the Assyrians (one of the people groups who speak Aramaic) got the concept of a "god of wealth" from their neighbors, the Babylonians.

Babylon was a city founded on pride and arrogance. The history of this pride goes all the way back to the account of the tower of Babel in Genesis 11. At its heart is an attitude that says: "We don't need God. We're self-sufficient." This is what the spirit of mammon tries to tell us, too. "You don't need God. Trust in riches!"

In the biblical sense of the word, mammon is the spirit that relies on money in our fallen world's system. Did you know that all money has some kind of spirit on it? It either has the Spirit of God on it because it has been redeemed and sanctified or it has the spirit of mammon.

Money that's submitted to God and His purposes has God's Spirit on it—which is why it multiplies and can't be consumed by the devourer. Money that has been submitted to God—wealth devoted to serving Him rather than trying to replace Him—is blessed by God. In a real sense, God's Spirit blesses it.

On the other hand, money that is not submitted to God has the spirit of mammon on it by default. That's why people so often try to use money to control or manipulate others. It's why people think money can bring them happiness or peace.

Mammon is basically the spirit of the world—and that spirit is a liar. As a result, people most under the influence of the spirit of mammon tend to have the most fear about their money. That's why Jesus said, "You cannot serve God and mammon" (Matthew 6:24). Mammon wants to rule. The spirit of mammon is looking for servants. It's seeking worshipers. It will promise you everything but can deliver nothing.

As Jesus suggests, mammon tries to take the very place of God. Pastor Jimmy Evans of Trinity Fellowship Church in Amarillo, Texas, once said, "Mammon promises us those things that only God can give—security, significance, identity, independence, power, and freedom. Mammon tells us it can insulate us from life's problems and that money is the answer to every situation."

When you think about it, mammon is nothing more than the system of this fallen world that stands in sharp opposition to God and His ways. For example, mammon says to buy and sell; God says to sow and reap. Mammon says to cheat and steal; God says to give and receive. But more than anything, mammon wants to rule.

It's no coincidence that in the book of Revelation, the Antichrist attempts to dominate people through the use of economics—preventing people from buying or selling unless they submit to him (Revelation 13:17). In this way, the brief rule of the Antichrist will be through the spirit of mammon.

Don't get the wrong idea. Money and mammon are not synonymous. Money is not inherently evil. One of the most frequently misquoted verses in the Bible is in 1 Timothy

6:10, "For the love of money is the root of all evil." Of course most people misquote this as "Money is the root of all evil."

The Bible warns us that the love of (or worship of) money is the root of all kinds of evil. It is the idolatrous love of the spirit of mammon that is evil. In other words, greed, covetousness, and selfishness are all manifestations of the spirit of mammon.

The reason we cannot serve both God and mammon is that the spirit of mammon is the opposite of the Spirit of God. Mammon says to take and hoard; God says to give and trust. Mammon is selfish; God is generous.

Sadly, unbelievers aren't the only ones susceptible to this kind of deception. Many times when believers are under extreme financial pressure, the spirit of mammon will slip up beside us. Then, it whispers that the solution to all our challenges is one of two things: We either need God to miraculously change our circumstances or we need someone to drop a truckload of money on us. This daydream usually involves an inheritance from a wealthy relative we didn't know about or winning the lottery, a contest, or sweepstakes. The real answer is never more money. The answer is always more of God.

NOTES

For group discussion or personal reflection:

QUESTION 1

How many prayers per day do you think God hears asking Him to bless the purchase of a lottery ticket by delivering a jackpot payout? What kind of "deals" and promises do you think accompany such prayers?

_____

_____

_____

_____

QUESTION 2

Mammon lies to us by promising those things that only God can give—security, significance, identity, independence, power, or freedom. In the past, which of these have you been most likely to believe that wealth could deliver?

_____

_____

_____

QUESTION 3

Money that has the Spirit of God on it cannot be touched by the devourer. God will protect and bless that money. Money that has the spirit of mammon on it, however, can and will be touched by the devourer. In what ways have you seen your money _devoured_ in the past?

_____

_____

_____

_____

QUESTION 4

Luke 16:10 suggests that only those who are faithful in small things should expect to be entrusted with bigger things. What are some of the "small things" with which we've been entrusted in life? And how can wise stewardship of those small things lead to bigger things?

_____

_____

_____

_____

QUESTION 5

God is looking for good stewards to whom He can entrust more resources, knowing such people will faithfully invest in saving souls, helping the hurting, and advancing His kingdom. What are some key characteristics of a good steward?

_____

_____

_____

_____

PRAY

Take some time as a group to lift one another up in the light of the truths discussed in this session.

Want to go deeper? Here is some food for thought, prayer, and journaling in the coming week.

KEY QUOTE

"God is the only one who can turn money into souls."   —Robert Morris

What can you change about your current financial stewardship that would enable you to invest more in people?

Teach those who are rich in this world not to be proud and not to trust in their money, which is so unreliable. Their trust should be in God, who richly gives us all we need for our enjoyment. Tell them to use their money to do good. They should be rich in good works and generous to those in need, always being ready to share with others. (1 Timothy 6:17, 18 NLT)

According to these verses, God wants to richly give us all we need to enjoy life as we trust Him and bless others. Write a few lines about what it is you truly need to enjoy life. What makes life good?

KEY VERSES

Luke 16:9-16, Romans 11:16, 1 Timothy 6:10

What stands out to you as you read these verses?

What is the Holy Spirit saying to you through these scriptures?

KEY QUESTION

If you are not going to derive your identity from how much and what kind of stuff you have, use Scripture to determine what *does* define your identity?

I am:	Scripture Reference:
e.g., A beloved child of God	Galatians 3:26
	II Corinthians 5:21
	Colossians 3:12
	Ephesians 1:6-8
	Romans 8:17

Add some of your own:

_____   _____

_____   _____

_____   _____

KEY PRAYER

Father, I recognize that You and You alone
are the source of my security, significance,
identity, independence, power, and freedom. Please break the hold of the spirit of
mammon on my life and finances as You
give me the grace to be a wise and faithful
steward. Help me remember that as I
demonstrate faithfulness in small things,
I will find myself entrusted with more.

NOTES

_____

_____

_____

_____

_____

_____

_____

_____

_____

_____

Am I Generous?

OUR HEARTS ARE A BATTLEGROUND ON WHICH SELFISHNESS AND GENEROSITY FIGHT FOR DOMINANCE.

RECAP

In the previous section, we explored the lies the spirit of mammon tells us about wealth—promising that more money will provide solutions to all of our problems. As you handled your finances this past week, in what ways have you been more aware of the subtle ways the spirit of mammon permeates our culture's attitudes about money and wealth?

ENGAGE

Many great movies have been built around the theme of generosity vs. selfishness. *It's a Wonderful Life, The Blind Side, A Christmas Carol, Pay It Forward, Schindler's List*, and *Casablanca* are just a few.

Pick one of these and talk about the ways generosity and selfishness are displayed in the film. Or, choose another favorite film in which generosity is a major theme and discuss its role in the film.

Watch Robert Morris' teaching titled "Am I Generous?" As you view it:

• Watch for the way we typically define "extravagance" in other people's lifestyles.

• Look for the three levels of giving described in the Bible.

(If you are not able to watch this teaching on DVD, read the following pages. Otherwise, skip to the TALK section after viewing.)

READ

It always makes sense to be generous toward God because He is always generous toward us. Actually, He is more than generous in His love toward us—He is extravagant.

A great biblical account of extravagant giving is found in John 12:1-8:

Then, six days before the Passover, Jesus came to Bethany, where Lazarus was who had been dead, whom He had raised from the dead. There they made Him a supper; and Martha served, but Lazarus was one of those who sat at the table with Him. Then Mary took a pound of very costly oil of spikenard, anointed the feet of Jesus, and wiped His feet with her hair. And the house was filled with the fragrance of the oil. But one of His disciples, Judas Iscariot, Simon's son, who would betray Him, said, "Why was this fragrant oil not sold for three hundred

> THIS INCIDENT HIGHLIGHTS THE FACT THAT WHEREVER YOU FIND GENEROSITY, YOU WILL FIND SELFISHNESS BATTLING AGAINST IT FOR CONTROL.

denarii and given to the poor?" This he said, not that
he cared for the poor, but because he was a thief,
and had the money box; and he used to take what
was put in it. But Jesus said, "Let her alone; she has
kept this for the day of My burial. For the poor
you have with you always, but Me you do not have
always."

This amazing story brings us a sharp contrast of two hearts. On one hand, we have the heart of Mary and on the other, the heart of Judas. In essence, we have both generosity and selfishness displayed for us in one incident.

Why did Mary do this? Why did she give such an extravagant, generous gift to the Lord? Three hundred denarii was a very large sum of money—basically the equivalent of an entire year's wages. Of course, what constitutes a lot of money is relative. What seems like a lot to the average person may not seem like much to a multimillionaire. But a year's income is a year's income, regardless of the tax bracket for which you qualify.

To get a feel for the magnitude of this gift, think about your annual household income and imagine spending that amount on some perfumed oil. Now, imagine taking it and pouring it onto someone's feet. You are never going to get it back. It's been poured out. It's gone.

What an extraordinary act! But it prompts the question: "Why?" And why did it bother Judas so much? After all, it wasn't his money.

This incident highlights the fact that wherever you find generosity, you will find selfishness battling against it for control. It was true in that situation and it is true in our own hearts. Each of us has to take a hard, inward look and ask these questions: Am I generous or am I selfish? Which of these attitudes has the upper hand in my life?

There's a breathtaking selfishness at work in Judas' heart in this account. It's manifested in his comments about Mary's offering. He didn't actually care for the poor. He was a thief! Judas pretended to be thinking about others while he was really only thinking of himself.

This same false spirituality manifests itself in similar comments we are likely to hear today. "How could anyone in good conscience drive a car that expensive?" "She sure could have helped a lot of people for what she spent on that purse." Or, "I sure could do a lot of good with the money they spent on that [insert name of item here]."

Remarks such as these are invariably envy, jealousy, and selfishness dressed up as religious superiority—and it's ugly.

This is exactly what Judas did on the day Mary anointed the feet of Jesus. Here was a year's wages being "wasted" instead of passing through the money box so that he could pilfer a good chunk of it. That's basically how Judas viewed a grateful woman's beautiful act of sacrificial worship —a waste.

A selfish person will sell out his or her friends if it will help that person get what he or she wants. And a selfish person will always, always find good reasons not to be generous.

Just as Judas did, selfishness tries to get the focus off of the selfish one and onto the "extravagance" of others. Mary came to Jesus with a heart overflowing with gratitude and love. That love translated itself into worship through an offering of great price.

In a similar way, we show God each week how much gratitude and love are in our hearts. So ask yourself some revealing questions: "What do my offerings say about my heart levels of gratitude and love for God? What does my spending say about what's truly important to me on this earth?"

There is battle raging inside each of us. It is a battle between selfishness and generosity; it is a battle generosity must win.

Real generosity is extravagant. But how can we ever hope to give an extravagant offering to the God of the universe? There is only one thing you can possibly give to God that would constitute an extravagant gift—yourself. You can offer up all you are and ever will be to Him.

NOTES

Talk

For group discussion or personal reflection:

QUESTION 1

As any parent can attest, children are born knowing how to be selfish. Selfishness comes naturally, but generosity must be learned and cultivated. Describe one of your earliest memories of wrestling with your own selfish nature.

QUESTION 2

We tend to find it easier to be generous in some areas of our lives than in others (e.g., time, money, possessions, credit for accomplishments, etc.). In what areas of life have you found it most difficult to be generous?

But without faith it is impossible to please Him, for he who comes to God must believe that He is, and that He is a rewarder of those who diligently seek Him (Hebrews 11:6).

QUESTION 3

This scripture declares that God's very nature is to be a "rewarder." Yet many believers instinctively view Him as essentially a withholder/punisher. Which has been your view in the past and why?

QUESTION 4

Describe an *extravagant* gift you have given to another person or received from someone. What made it extravagant? What was the impact?

QUESTION 5

When the Holy Spirit prompts you to give an extravagant gift to the Lord or to His work, what kinds of emotions and thoughts tend to rush in to discourage you from obeying?

PRAY

Take some time as a group to lift one another up in the light of the truths discussed in this session.

Want to go deeper? Here is some food for thought, prayer, and journaling in the coming week.

KEY QUOTE

"Hebrews says God is a rewarder. He'll not only give you what's normal for tithing, He'll give you over and above. If you'll give with the right heart, God is going to reward you, and I'm sorry but I can't stop it. I can't do anything about it, because it's His nature. He's a rewarder." —Robert Morris

Read the following scriptures and write in your own words what is being said about God's desire and ability to be your . . .

Promoter (Psalm 5:12; Psalm 75:6, 7; James 4:10)

_____

_____

_____

Protector (Psalm 4:8; Psalm 121:3; Proverbs 18:10; Luke 10:19)

_____

_____

_____

Provider (Psalm 111:5; Matthew 6:33; 2 Corinthians 9:10; Philippians 4:19)

_____

_____

_____

KEY VERSES

John 12:1-8, Proverbs 11:25, 2 Corinthians 8:3-5

What stands out to you as you read these verses?

What is the Holy Spirit saying to you through these scriptures?

KEY QUESTION

Have you given God an extravagant gift?

The most extravagant gift you can give God is *you*. Indeed, giving yourself wholly and fully to God from a heart overflowing with gratitude is the only gift you can hope to give that will "impress" God.

The lyrics of the chorus of Phillips, Craig & Dean's song, *I Pour My Love On You*, recalls Mary's extravagant gift:

Like oil upon your feet
Like wine for you to drink
Like water from my heart
I pour my love on you
If praise is like perfume
I lavish mine on you
Till every drop is gone
I'll pour my love on you

Write your own hymn or letter of
consecration and gratitude to God.

_____

_____

_____

_____

_____

_____

_____

_____

_____

_____

KEY PRAYER

Father, I recognize that You are the only real
source of promotion, protection, and provi-
sion in my life. You gave the unbelievably
extravagant gift of Your own Son so I could
know You, be whole, have abundant life,
and be with You forever. Please give me a
deeper revelation of all You have given me.
And in the light of that revelation, create in
me an extravagantly generous heart.

NOTES

_____

_____

_____

_____

_____

The Principles of Multiplication
part 1

THE MIRACLE OF MULTIPLICATION IS AVAILABLE TO GOD'S PEOPLE. BUT WHAT WE HAVE MUST BE "BLESSED" BY JESUS BEFORE IT CAN MULTIPLY. AND MULTIPLICATION COMES THROUGH SHARING.

Engage

RECAP

In the previous section, we explored the power of extravagant giving springing from a heart of generosity. Were there any moments this last week in which you were reminded that God is our Promoter, Protector, and Provider?

ENGAGE

You're going to host a big meal for a large group of friends or family. What's on the menu?

Watch Robert Morris' teaching titled "The Principles of Multiplication—Part 1" As you view it:

• Look for the way in which Jesus' miracle of multiplying of the loaves and fish happened differently than we typically assume.

• Watch for the first key to multiplication of resources.

(If you are not able to watch this teaching on DVD, read the following pages. Otherwise, skip to the TALK section after viewing.)

READ

God is a multiplier. He multiplied oil and meal for a poor widow and her son. He multiplied the strength of outnumbered Israelite soldiers in battle after battle. And He multiplied fish and loaves on a couple of Galilean hillsides. Clearly, God is the master of multiplication.

In Luke 9:12-17 we find the account of one of those miraculous multiplications—the feeding of the 5,000 households:

When the day began to wear away, the twelve came and said to Him, "Send the multitude away, that they may go into the surrounding towns and country, and lodge and get provisions; for we are in a deserted place here." But He said to them, "You give them something to eat." And they said, "We

> THIS IS WHAT WE HAVE MISSED IN THIS REMARK-ABLE STORY. THE MIRACLE DIDN'T HAPPEN IN THE MASTER'S HANDS—IT HAPPENED IN THE DISCIPLES' HANDS.

*have no more than five loaves and two fish, unless
we go and buy food for all these people." For there
were about five thousand men.*

*Then He said to His disciples, "Make them sit down
in groups of fifty." And they did so, and made them
all sit down. Then He took the five loaves and the
two fish, and looking up to heaven, He blessed and
broke them, and gave them to the disciples to set
before the multitude. So they all ate and were filled,
and twelve baskets of the leftover fragments were
taken up by them.*

Notice after He blessed the food, Jesus began
breaking it in half and handing it to the disciples.
Can you imagine what someone like Peter was
thinking as he looked down at that half piece of
bread? He had handed Jesus a whole piece and
only got back half!

We have to wonder if Peter, looking down at that
little fragment, might have said to the Lord, "Um,
are you sure you're through praying? Wouldn't you
like to pray a little more? The Lord might have said,
"No, I've blessed it. Now go give it away."

Peter walked away with that half piece of bread in
His hand and obediently broke it in half the same
way he had seen Jesus do. Handing out chunks
of bread, he broke it in half again and again and
again. This is what we have missed in this remarkable story. The miracle didn't happen in the Master's
hands—it happened in the disciples' hands.

You know the outcome. With each of the disciples
duplicating this pattern, the result was twelve big
baskets of leftovers. Embodied in this real-life ac-

count are two very important principles for us. They represent two spiritual keys to multiplication in the kingdom of God.

This is the first principle: Something must be blessed before it can be multiplied.

When we give the first of our increase—the tithe—to the Lord, the rest of it is blessed. Remember the words of Romans 11: "For if the firstfruit is holy, the lump is also holy; and if the root is holy, so are the branches" (v. 16).

> THERE IS A DIFFERENCE BETWEEN TITHING AND GIVING. TITHING IS SIMPLY RETURNING TO GOD THAT WHICH HE SAID IS HIS.

Many sweet Christians have never seen their finances multiply. Often the reason is that their money hasn't been blessed. When you give it to the Lord first and the Lord puts His blessing on it, then—and only then—does it have the ability to multiply.

Jesus—the One who receives our tithes—is the only One who has the power to bless our money so it can multiply. That's the first principle of multiplication.

This is the second principle: Only what is given away can multiply.

In the example of the miraculous feeding in the Galilean countryside, the disciples held the bread and the fish. It had been blessed, so it had the potential to multiply. But if they had just eaten themselves, it would have remained five loaves and two fish. It would never have multiplied—even though Jesus Himself had blessed it! They would have each had a couple of bites of food instead of full stomachs and twelve baskets of leftovers.

They had to give it away so it could multiply.

This is another reason many believers never see the miracle of multiplication in their finances. Sometimes those who are tithing give little or nothing over and above the tithe. They don't realize that only that which is given away can multiply.

There is a difference between tithing and giving. Tithing is simply returning to God that which He said is His. Giving our firstfruits—our first ten percent to the Lord via a local church—is what causes that which is ours to be blessed.

You can't "give" that which doesn't really belong to you. The firstfruits belong to the Lord. The rest is yours to keep or give as you choose. It is from this account that you give what the Bible often refers to as offerings.

Tithing isn't really giving—it's returning. It is bringing back to the Lord what is already His. Thus, the second principle of multiplication is that finances must be shared if they are to multiply.

NOTES

For group discussion or personal reflection:

QUESTION 1

What does the miracle of the fish and loaves tell us about God's concern about our material needs?

QUESTION 2

Why do you think Jesus instructed the disciples to divide the huge crowd into groups of 50? What areas of your life might require some organization and order before God can bring increase to them?

QUESTION 3

Only that which has been "blessed" by the Lord can multiply. The disciples put the loaves and fish into Jesus hands so He could bless them. How can we put the money that comes to us into Jesus' hands so He can bless it? (Read Hebrews 7:8.)

_____

_____

_____

_____

Describe a time when you have seen the principle
of multiplication at work in your life or in the life of
someone you know?

_____

_____

_____

_____

_____

QUESTION 5

Tithing is bringing to God that which is rightfully
His. It is when we give over and above the tithe that
the miracle of multiplication takes place. How do
you decide when, where, and how much to give?

_____

_____

_____

_____

PRAY

Take some time as a group to lift one another up in
the light of the truths discussed in this session.

Want to go deeper? Here is some food for thought, prayer, and journaling in the coming week.

KEY QUOTE

"What if the disciples had given the fish and the loaves out without Jesus blessing it? It never would have multiplied. It was the blessing of Jesus that gave it the potential to multiply. There are many, many people who give a little here, and give a little there. But they never see their finances multiplied, and the reason is they're not blessed by Jesus."   —Robert Morris

Describe the last time you can recall God speaking to you about giving a significant gift over and above your tithe to a person or ministry; describe your response.

God asked me to . . .

_____

_____

_____

And I . . .

_____

_____

_____

_____

What emotional, spiritual, or practical factors may be keeping you from giving more frequently and more generously, e.g., fear, busyness, excessive debt.

How, with God's help and wisdom, can you address those obstacles?

KEY VERSES
Proverbs 22:9, John 12:24, 25, Romans 11:16, 2 Corinthians 9:5-11

What stands out to you as you read these verses?

What is the Holy Spirit saying to you through these scriptures?

KEY QUESTION

Are your finances blessed? And do you trust God enough to obey when He says give, even when it doesn't seem there will be enough to go around? Why or why not?

KEY PRAYER

Father, You are the one who multiplied the courage of a shepherd boy when he was facing a giant, multiplied the strength of Samson when he took on an army, multiplied oil and meal for a widow in Zarephath, and multiplied a boy's lunch in the hands of Jesus and His disciples. Please give me the faith and courage to place my resources in Your hands and to distribute them freely as You instruct me so that I might experience the miracle of multiplication with all You have entrusted to me.

NOTES

The Principles of Multiplication
part 2

GOD IS LOOKING FOR AUDACIOUS, COURAGEOUS, EXTRAVAGANT GIVERS WHO TRUST HIM AND UNDERSTAND THE INCREASE – PRODUCING POWER OF THE PRINCIPLES OF MULTIPLICATION.

RECAP

In the previous section, we were challenged to be listening for the voice of the Holy Spirit prompting us to give courageously. In the past week, have you been presented with any such promptings? What happened?

ENGAGE

What is the worst car you have ever driven? What made it so awful?

Watch Robert Morris' teaching titled "The Principles of Multiplication—Part 2" As you view it:

• Look for three things Robert and Debbie Morris did to get their "financial house" in order.

• Watch for the remarkable opportunity God only offers to "extravagant givers."

(If you are not able to watch this teaching on DVD, read the following pages. Otherwise, skip to the TALK section after viewing.)

READ

As a full-time traveling evangelist back in the 1980s, Robert Morris' entire income came from the love offerings he received from the churches in which he preached. In those years, his income from offerings might be $800 one week and $200 the next. He and his wife, Debbie, just never knew what they would be given. But early in their marriage, they learned to trust God where their finances were concerned.

The Lord spoke clearly to them about getting their finances in order—getting out and staying out of debt, living within their means, and refusing to manipulate others for their own gain.

They were also diligent tithers. God had spoken clearly to them about the principle of the tithe. Ever since they honored the

IN ONE MEET-ING, GOD MIRACULOUSLY PROVIDED WHAT IT NORMALLY TOOK SEVERAL MEETINGS TO PRODUCE. IT WAS QUITE A LESSON FOR THE YOUNG EVANGELIST.

Lord by giving the first tenth of everything that came in, their needs were always met—sometimes miraculously. What they didn't know was that God was about to take them to the next level.

Robert was scheduled to preach only one night at a certain church. As it turned out, it was the only meeting he was scheduled to preach all month long. From a financial standpoint, that meant he had only one opportunity to receive an offering instead of the usual four, five or six. Although he and Debbie had grown in their ability to trust and rest in God, this was a major budgeting challenge in the making.

The night of the meeting came. At the close of the service, the church received a love offering on Robert's behalf. Shortly thereafter, the pastor approached him with an envelope.

He said, "Robert, I'm pleased and amazed to tell you that this is the largest love offering this little church has ever given. God used you to bless us tonight, and I'm so happy to be able to give this to you."

When he opened the envelope, he found a check for roughly the same amount as his entire monthly budget. In one meeting, God had miraculously provided what it normally took several meetings to produce. It was quite a lesson for the young evangelist. But the lesson wasn't over yet.

As he stood there holding that check, basking in the warm glow of gratitude and wonder, something happened that forever changed the course and quality of Robert's life.

Earlier in that evening's service, a missionary had

given a brief testimony and update for the congregation. As he looked across the nearly empty sanctuary, Robert caught a glimpse of the missionary. As he did, the unmistakable voice of the Lord spoke in his heart, "I want you to give him your offering—all of it."

In an instant, he went from euphoria to something approximating panic. "Lord that can't be your voice," he argued. "I mean . . . after all . . . I . . . You . . . You just did a miracle here to meet our needs!"

Once again, the instruction came through, gently but clearly, "I want you to give him your offering."

Like a kid who doesn't want to hear what his brother is saying, Robert wanted to stick his fingers in his ears and sing loudly, "La, La, La, La, La . . . what? I can't hear you!"

"Give him the whole offering. Trust me."

He couldn't shake it off. He tried to rationalize. He tried bargaining. The impression only grew stronger.

Ultimately, he waved the white flag and said, "Okay, Father, I trust You." He endorsed the back of the check, folded it in half, and took a quick glance around the room to make sure no one was watching.

Walking up to the missionary, he said something like, "I really appreciated your testimony tonight. Please, don't tell anyone about this, but I would like you to have this offering. The check is made out to me, but I've signed it over to you." He handed him the check and walked away.

An hour later he found himself seated with about a dozen members of the church at a pizza place. Across from him sat a well-dressed man he had met briefly on a previous occasion.

After a while, the man leaned across the table toward Robert, looked him straight in the eye, and asked a shockingly personal question: "How much was your offering tonight?"

Understandably, this question flustered Robert. He had never had anyone ask him that before, especially a near stranger. The man's boldness so caught him off guard that Robert didn't know what else to do but answer him. He told the man the amount of the offering check, hoping that was the end of the matter. It wasn't.

In the same authoritative manner, the man followed up with another question: "Where is the check?"

What nerve! Robert remembered thinking. *What is this guy up to?*

Of course, Robert no longer had the check, but he wasn't about to tell this gentleman about that. Still flustered and off balance, Robert lied.

"Uh . . . my wife has it."

Debbie was sitting with some of the other wives at the other end of the long table—a nice, safe distance away. *Now can we change the subject?* he thought.

"Go get it. I want to see it," said the man.

The man was relentless! Not knowing what else to do, Robert made a pretense of getting up to go ask her for the check. Bending down close to her ear, he asked, "How's your pizza?"

"Good," she replied, giving Robert a perplexed look.

"Great. Glad to hear it. Just checking," he muttered and headed back to his seat.

Robert's ears heard another lie floating past his lips. "She left it out in the car," Robert said, trying to make the car sound as if it was very, very far away. Robert also recalls that at this point, he was not only trying to hide the fact that he had given his entire love offering away to a stranger but was also covering the fact that the evangelist who had just spent the evening proclaiming that Jesus is the way, the truth, and the life had just lied!

As tiny beads of perspiration began to pop out on Robert's face, the gentleman leaned across the table and got uncomfortably close.

"The check's not in the car, Robert," he stated in a low voice.

"How do you know that?" Robert responded, trying not to sound a little offended.

"Because God told me—and He told me

THE MAN SPOKE WORDS THAT HAVE ROLLED LIKE THUNDER THROUGH ROBERT'S LIFE EVER SINCE: "GOD IS ABOUT TO TEACH YOU ABOUT GIVING SO THAT YOU CAN TEACH THE BODY OF CHRIST."

something else." At that point, the man spoke words that have rolled like thunder through Robert's life ever since: "God is about to teach you about giving so that you can teach the Body of Christ."

With that, the man pulled out a piece of paper and showed it to Robert. It was a check. The amount—to the penny—was ten times the amount of the one he had given away only an hour earlier.

Ten times—to the penny. It was a miracle of multiplication.

The man's words stayed at the forefront of Robert and Debbie's minds in the amazing months that followed that night at the pizza parlor. They were wide open to anything God wanted to teach them. And as a result, they saw the principle of multiplication at work in their financial lives time and again.

NOTES

_____

_____

_____

_____

_____

_____

_____

_____

_____

For group discussion or personal reflection:

QUESTION 1

When we give the first tenth to the Lord, the remaining nine-tenths is blessed and has the capacity to multiply when we give it as the Holy Spirit directs. Nevertheless, surveys reveal that few believers even tithe, much less give over and above. Why do you think this is so?

QUESTION 2

"I can't afford to tithe," and "I don't have anything to give," are common statements among Christians. What practical steps can be taken to overcome these obstacles?

QUESTION 3

Has anyone ever given you something because the Lord instructed him or her to do so? Describe the experience.

_____

_____

QUESTION 4

Hearing the Lord instruct you to give something—a car, a specific sum of money, or some other possession—obviously requires the ability to hear God's voice. Do you currently hear His voice at that level? In what ways can we become more sensitive to prompting and instructions from the Lord?

_____

_____

_____

_____

PRAY

Take some time as a group to lift one another up in light of the truths discussed in this session.

NOTES

_____

_____

_____

_____

_____

_____

_____

_____

Want to go deeper? Here is some food for thought, prayer, and journaling in the coming week.

KEY QUOTE

"Years ago God spoke to us to get our finances in order. By the way, you can't be a giver unless you get your finances in order. He told me three things that were specific to my finances . . . He said, 'Number one, get out of debt' . . . 'the second thing He said to me was 'Don't manipulate others [concerning money]' . . . the third thing the Lord told me was 'Give.' The Lord said, 'I want you to begin to give extravagantly as I tell you to.'" —Robert Morris

Getting your finances in order.

Rank yourself on a scale of 1-10 (1 being the "worst" and 10 being "best") in the following areas:

AREA	SCORE
Getting (and staying) out of debt	
Living within your means	
Having a budget/tracking expenses	
Praying about significant purchases	
Being accountable in your spending (e.g., to spouse)	
Being diligent and faithful at work	

Manipulation

Ask the Lord to reveal to you any areas in which you tend to manipulate others concerning money or material things. Describe them briefly and how you could handle them differently by trusting in God.

Giving

Imagine your income doubled overnight. How could you use the additional income to invest in God's kingdom or bless others? Where or to whom would you give?

Now ask yourself, "What could I do *right now* to begin giving in these areas?"

KEY VERSES
Matthew 25:14-29,
Luke 16:9-13

What stands out to you as you read these verses?

_____

_____

_____

What is the Holy Spirit saying to you through these scriptures?

_____

_____

_____

_____

_____

KEY QUESTION

What if you clearly heard the Lord ask you for everything—all your savings, assets, and wealth? Write a prayer of response:

_____

_____

_____

_____

KEY PRAYER

Father, make me "blessable!" Please build in me a grateful, audacious, courageous, generous heart to give; for I know that this is the only way to experience fulfillment, purpose, joy, and peace in fullest measure. This is the key to living the blessed life.

NOTES

Leader's Guide

THE BLESSED LIFE LEADER'S GUIDE IS DESIGNED TO HELP YOU BETTER LEAD YOUR SMALL GROUP OR CLASS THROUGH *THE BLESSED LIFE* CURRICULUM. USE THIS GUIDE ALONG WITH THE CURRICULUM FOR A LIFE-CHANGING, INTERACTIVE EXPERIENCE.

BEFORE YOU MEET:

- Ask God to prepare the hearts and minds of the people in your group. Ask Him to show you how to encourage each person to integrate the principles you discover into their daily lives through group discussion and personal journaling.

- Preview the DVD segment for the week.

- Plan how much time you'll allot to each portion of your meeting (see suggested schedule below). In case you're unable to get through them all in the time you have planned, here is a list of the most important questions (from the TALK section) for each week. These questions are also marked in the Participant Guide with the orange arrow.

SESSION ONE

Q: Generosity flows easily and naturally from a heart of gratitude. What are some practical ways to cultivate a more grateful heart toward God?

SESSION TWO

Q: Hebrews 7:8 suggests that when we tithe here on earth, Jesus spiritually receives those tithes in heaven. How does that knowledge impact your heart attitude as you bring your tithes and offerings?

Q: Have you tended to view tithing as a burden or a benefit? What practical steps could you take to keep yourself mindful of the benefits of tithing?

SESSION THREE

Q: Every time we are paid, an inescapable moment of "worship" immediately follows. The first place to which we direct a portion of that money reveals something about what is "first" in our lives. What kinds of financial things are most likely to compete for "first place" in our hearts?

Q: A 2007 survey by the Barna organization revealed that among Americans who had "prayed, read the Bible, and attended a church service in the previous week," only 12% made a regular practice of tithing. Why do you think that this one area proves so difficult for Bible-believing, church-going people?

SESSION FOUR

Q: Mammon lies to us by promising those things that only God can give—security, significance, identity, independence, power, or freedom. In the past, which of these have you been most likely to believe that wealth could deliver?

Q: Luke 16:10 suggests that only those who are faithful in small things should expect to be entrusted with bigger things. What are some of the "small things" with which we've been entrusted in life? How can wise stewardship of those small things lead to bigger things?

SESSION FIVE

Q: This scripture declares that God's very nature is to be a "rewarder," yet many believers instinctively view Him as essentially a withholder/punisher. Which has been your view in the past and why?

Q: When the Holy Spirit prompts you to give an extravagant gift to the Lord or to His work, what kinds of emotions and thoughts tend to rush in to discourage you from obeying?

SESSION SIX

Q: Only that which has been "blessed" by the Lord can multiply. The disciples put the loaves and fish into Jesus hands so He could bless them. How can we put the money that comes to us into Jesus' hands so He can bless it? (Read Hebrews 7:8.)

Q: Describe a time when you have seen the principle of multiplication at work in your life or in the life of someone you know.

SESSION SEVEN

Q: "I can't afford to tithe," and "I don't have anything to give," are common statements among Christians. What practical steps can be taken to overcome these obstacles?

Q: Hearing the Lord instruct you to give something—a car, a specific sum of money, or some other possession— obviously requires the ability to hear God's voice. Do you currently hear His voice at that level? In what ways can we become more sensitive to prompting and instructions from the Lord?

Remember, the goal is not necessarily to get through all of the questions. The highest priority is for the group to learn and engage in dynamic discussion.

HOW TO USE THE CURRICULUM:

- This study has a simple design. Each week:

  THE ONE THING — This is a single statement under each session title that sums up the main point—the key idea—of the session.

  RECAP — Recap the previous week's session, inviting members to share about any opportunities they encountered throughout the week to apply what they learned. (This doesn't apply to the first week.)

  ENGAGE — Ask the icebreaker question to help get people talking and feeling comfortable with one another.

  WATCH — Watch the included DVD (recommended).

  READ — If you're unable to watch the DVD, read the introduction.

  TALK — Discuss the questions.

  PRAY — Pray together.

  MEMORIZE — Encourage members to work on a memory verse.

  EXPLORE — Encourage members to complete the journal portion before the next meeting.

- Generate participation and discussion.

Resist the urge to teach. Ask open-ended questions—questions that can't be answered with "yes" or "no" (e.g., "What do you think about that?" rather than "Do you agree?"). When a question arises, ask the group for their input instead of answering it yourself right off the bat. Be comfortable with silence. If you ask a question and no one responds, rephrase the question and wait for a response. Your primary role is to create an environment where people feel comfortable to be themselves and participate, not to provide the answers to all of their questions.

• Ask the group to pray for each other from week to week, especially about key issues that arise during your group time. This is how you begin to build authentic community and encourage spiritual growth within the group.

SUGGESTED SCHEDULE FOR THE GROUP:

1. ENGAGE and RECAP (5 minutes)
2. WATCH and READ (15 minutes)
3. TALK (35-45 minutes)
4. PRAY (10 minutes)

KEYS TO A DYNAMIC SMALL GROUP:

Relationships
Meaningful, encouraging relationships are the foundation of a dynamic small group. Teaching, discussion, worship, and prayer are important elements of a group meeting, but the depth of each element is often dependent upon the depth of the relationships between members.

Availability
Building a sense of community within your group requires members to prioritize their relationships with one another. This means being available to listen, care for one another, and meet each other's needs.

Mutual Respect

Mutual respect is shown when members value others' opinions (even when they disagree) and are careful to never belittle or embarrass others in the group (including their spouses, who may or may not be present).

Openness

A healthy small group environment encourages sincerity and transparency. Members treat each other with grace in areas of weakness, allowing each other room to grow.

Confidentiality

To develop authenticity and a sense of safety within the group, each member must be able to trust that things discussed within the group will not be shared outside the group.

Shared Responsibility

Group members will share the responsibility of group meetings by using their God-given abilities to serve at each gathering. Some may greet, some may host, some may teach, etc. Ideally, each person should be available to care for one another as needed.

Sensitivity

Dynamic small groups are born when the leader consistently seeks and is responsive to the guidance of the Holy Spirit, following His leading throughout the meeting as opposed to sticking to the "agenda." This is especially important during the discussion and ministry time.

Fun!

Dynamic small groups take the time to have fun! Create an atmosphere for fun, and be willing to laugh at yourself every now and then!

2-14-14 Prayer / Praise :
- Alice → friend had miscarriage.
- Chantel (Alice's daughter (adopted))
- Ronica's family - uncle passed away
- Shannon's dad - travel; mom safety ; TCA
- Alice's aunt in Puerto Rico health & spiritual
  life
- Ronica praise - friend in Denver - brain
  tumor and anyerism - Merlin - doing
  well after surgery and at home now.
- Sharon - property tax bill - it is
  payed in her mortgage - praise !
- AJ is taking SAT's on March 8.
- Vivian having surgery on March 3.

2-21-14 Prayer / Praise :
- Gigi → looking for a job. Had a job
  interview today.
- Debra → Ronica's customer - depression,
  takes meds to get out of her house.
- Shannon's mom - praise
             dad - travel
          money for bills

NOTES

NOTES

NOTES

NOTES

NOTES

NOTES

CPSIA information can be obtained at www.ICGtesting.com
Printed in the USA
LVOW01s2324160713

343238LV00010B/12/P